Highly sensitive & emotional children

How to lovingly accompany, educate, encourage and strengthen your child - Highly sensitive and happy

Maria Groninga

CONTENT

What you can expect in this book

A child is a sensitive little thing! - Yes, and?! What's wrong with that? Maybe your child even belongs to the group of highly sensitive people. Unfortunately, however, "being sensitive" is often pronounced with a negative undertone. You may have noticed that your child perceives certain stimuli, no matter on what level, particularly intensively or even more readily than you do. It could also be that your child withdraws more often, wants to be to himself or herself, or screams and rages loudly from one second to the next. But does that make your child a "highly sensitive child"? And if so, how can you deal with it and accompany and support it in its special emotional life? Do you raise a highly sensitive child differently? Questions regarding the daycare center routine or the school experience for highly sensitive children are also answered in this book. In addition, you will become part of a process that begins with yourself and is intended to bring you closer to your child.

Elaine Aron, who has been instrumental in getting more attention to high sensitivity, once said the following:

"To raise an extraordinary child, you have to be willing to commit to an extraordinary child."

By informing yourself here now, you are already starting to get involved in the topic of high sensitivity. If you then suspect that your child is highly sensitive, approach your pediatrician or inform yourself at the appropriate associations.

1. at what point does one speak of high sensitivity?

Before we get into what it means to be highly sensitive, let's first look at what the term "sensitive" means. The term comes from Latin and is translated as "sensitive". If we take a look at the Duden here, sensitive is also defined with sensitive and, in addition, that a person has a special sensitivity. In addition, however, there is also the explanation "sensitive to pain and stimuli from the outside". The following terms, among others, are mentioned as synonyms: sensitive, subtle, tactful, respectful.

1.1 ORIGIN OF THE HIGH SENSITIVITY

The term high sensitivity is not yet very widespread and was only recognized and conceptually defined by Elaine Aron in a study in 1991. Even though there were observations in this area before, it was Aron who coined the term.

In an interview conducted over three hours with 40 people, regardless of gender, age and social background, basic characteristics were to be found out. These interviews served as the basis for a questionnaire that was carried out with over a thousand people. It is still possible to fill in such a questionnaire today. However, self-diagnosis is not recommended and a professional exchange with a psychologist is recommended.

It is estimated that up to 20% of all people are highly sensitive. It is assumed that highly sensitive people per se have a lower stimulus threshold and that this therefore also represents a biological disposition. However, it cannot be taken for granted that it is hereditary.

Rather, it is a genetic predisposition that may or may not blossom.

1.2 CAUSES

But where does this high sensitivity come from? In fact, your child is already born with it. It is a predisposition and thus often genetically pre-programmed. Thus, highly sensitive people are always found in a family in a straight line. However, trauma can also lead to high sensitivity.

The nervous system is particularly receptive and sensitive and the reflexes are also significantly more active, which means that pain is felt more strongly. All this knowledge was proven in a neuroscientific study in 2011. It was also stated that highly sensitive people are not shy per se. This can also be added only when the environment can not deal with it appropriately and then those affected people withdraw.

All these explanations remain so far rather conjectures, because the field of high sensitivity is still very young and many questions are open. A lot of research is being done on what and how this phenomenon manifests itself, but the causes have so far been given rather little attention.

1.3 BEING HIGHLY SENSITIVE - OR SIMPLY FEELING A LOT

Is my child now highly sensitive because he or she simply can't handle stimuli that well? Let's take a look at what constitutes high sensitivity in general.

High sensitivity is a disposition. The sensory organs do not differ from other children. Your child comes into the world with this temperament trait.

"Every day is like a fair for me." "Just smelling my husband's deodorant gives me a migraine." "The noise of the computer in the neighbor's office drives me crazy." This is a small insight of statements of highly sensitive people.

First of all, it can be stated quite simply that stimuli are perceived more intensively and thus also processed in a more varied manner. Feelings and senses are activated in a more direct way. This intensity is significantly stronger than usual, which in turn often makes those people appear "different". Neurologically, highly sensitive people perform an enormous amount of processing in the brain. Everything that is taken in as impressions is sorted, evaluated, analyzed in its unbelievable quantity and variety and only then passed on as information. There is no primary sorting out - every sound, every smell, simply everything is absorbed, processed and passed on. This already sounds incredibly exhausting and is also described as a phenomenon by neurologists.

High sensitivity should be seen as a gift. Anyone who can perceive so much is special, but of course is also very influenced and affected by it in his everyday life. A previously unsorted flood of impressions must eventually also be processed, which in turn can lead at some point to the brain being overloaded. This is referred to as overstimulation.

In addition to a lack of selection of impressions of any kind, highly sensitive people also find it difficult to set priorities. What is important? Every smallest task is completed very conscientiously, or rather, perfectly. But this is also a big disadvantage when it comes to tasks that have to be checked off quickly. The courage to leave gaps is unthinkable for a highly sensitive person.

Thus, it can be stated that highly sensitive people perceive fine nuances earlier than others, which can be a clear advantage. On the other hand, however, they can quickly become overwhelmed because so many impressions are absorbed unfiltered.

Before we take a closer look at the positive effects of high sensitivity, but also at overstimulation in children, it should be shown how high sensitivity is differentiated from autism and AD(H)S. Since similar behavioral characteristics occur here again and again, the differen ciation is of great importance for adequate support.

1.4. DIFFERENCE FROM ASPERGER'S AUTISM

It is possible that certain facts and behaviors that have been described so far about highly sensitive individuals remind you of people with Asperger's autism. It is very difficult to clearly distinguish these two phenomena. To begin with, Asperger's syndrome is a disorder. It can be diagnosed medically, as there are standardized tests. In contrast, high sensitivity is a personality trait. Nevertheless, both are genetically predisposed. In comparison, more boys have Asperger's syndrome than girls. In the case of high sensitivity, there is no gender that is more likely to have high sensitivity. What is common to both is that they have a special attention to detail, that challenging situations can be overwhelming, or that social encounters are not easily managed. It is speculated that many Asperger's autistic people also show high sensitivity, but the other way around this is not so often the case. There is no clear boundary to be drawn here.

People with Asperger's autism often feel like strangers on this planet and have their very own world of feelings and thoughts that is difficult for outsiders to understand. Highly sensitive people also have to struggle with overstimulation, but they can deal with it more skillfully than Asperger's autistic people. Likewise, they can converse well and actually like to converse with other people and like social contact. Linguistically, both groups stand out. A child with Asperger's autism uses a rather unusual vocabulary that is not typical for their age, and their grammar is also often exaggerated. A highly sensitive child, on the other hand, surprises on the content level in their narratives. Especially with familiar people, they really blossom. Yes, closeness is a big issue for highly sensitive people, but they can always deal with it somehow. Both have in common that they usually have few friends, that they think a lot in pictures, love rituals, these are helpful for them, and both can only decide with great difficulty.

A very clear difference is the ability to empathize. While Asperger's autistic people have very little, if any, of this ability, highly sensitive people can empathize and empathize with others very well. Sometimes this is even almost too much. Likewise, it is precisely the great gift that highly sensitive people perceive the finest interpersonal nuances in facial expressions, gestures, pitches, etc.. An Asperger's autistic person cannot do that. Thus, a child with Asperger's autism needs clear rules because they are always taken literally. Highly sensitive children are able to understand irony, notice procedures and recognize rules even if they are not written down anywhere.

For example, if a child shows a strong discomfort with materials, consistencies, or even physical proximity, this is often a characteristic of Asperger's autism. However, highly sensitive children may also exhibit this characteristic. Since Asperger's autism can be diagnosed with the help of tests, it is quite possible to make sure if you suspect this in your child. Proceed with sensitivity, since your child already feels or thinks that something may be wrong with him or her.

1.5 DIFFERENCE TO AD(H)S

It is not uncommon that high sensitivity is often also mentioned when talking about AD(H)S. Nevertheless, both characteristics are defined and named separately. Children with AD(H)S and highly sensitive children have in common that they are very sensitive to the stimuli of their everyday life. Likewise, both groups have to adapt enormously on a daily basis in order to cope to some extent in our fast-paced and stimulus-flooded world. They are confronted with having to fit into norms and expected performances and, in addition, to process their own emotional life and their perception of other people and, if necessary, to constantly balance themselves and remain relaxed.

It is not very easy to distinguish the two phenomena right away when you have suspicions about a child. One difference, however, is that children with AD(H)S find it very difficult to focus and do so constantly. Even when everything around him is quiet, this child cannot focus. A highly sensitive child, on the other hand, is a master at concentration. They can handle topics and tasks with great care and perseverance. Highly sensitive children also find it easier to implement what they have already learned and do so without help. Children with AD(H)S are significantly longer or even permanently dependent on help here. If both children are distracted by a strong stimulus, a child with AD(H)S finds it difficult or even impossible to return to the original task. Highly sensitive children can also be distracted, but can then pick up where they left off. If a highly sensitive child is under pressure and stress arises, they may show similar behavior to a child with AD(H)S. They may also become agitated and restless. Then they also become restless and the focus cannot be maintained.

Another difference becomes clear when it comes to both children having to tidy something up. Highly sensitive children tidy up very orderly, it seems as if they have an inner logic. Highly sensitive children like it very much when things are tidy. For children with AD(H)S, tidying up is a very big challenge. If a toy falls into their hands during this process that gets their attention, they no longer know that they are supposed to be cleaning up and want to play. In everyday school life, both children are conspicuous because they do not participate in what is going on. The difference, however, is that highly sensitive children like to daydream away, think a lot, and they try to classify impressions and then also process them. Children with AD(H)S tend to show erratic behavior. As described in the case of tidying up, something else can please them very quickly and then they have to play with it, for example. In addition, these children also consciously look for variety and actively start something new. In general, one cannot exclude that a child with AD(H)S can also be highly sensitive. The other way around, however, this is again rather rarely the case. Thus, high sensitivity can be a characteristic for AD(H)S.

- High sensitivity is genetically predisposed.

- High sensitivity is a temperament trait.

- It is assumed that up to 20% of all people are highly sensitive.

- Highly sensitive people perceive particularly intensively. This can refer to sounds, touch, smells, temperature, materials and much more. Likewise, they can perceive all these things intensively or only one of them. The expression can be very individual.

- All external impressions are absorbed and processed unfiltered - this is incredibly stressful for highly sensitive people.

- Overstimulation occurs when a highly sensitive person has no opportunity to calm down or withdraw. This concentrated flood of impressions that must be processed is simply too much at a certain point.

- There are similarities between high sensitivity and AD(H)S and also Asperger's autism. It should be tried to delimit this, best with a psychologist, in order to be able to accompany and act individually suitable.

2. how does high sensitivity manifest itself in children?

A baby who wants to stay in the sling without interruption, a never-ending settling-in period at daycare, an exhausted child after a children's birthday party ... these could also be normal sensitive children at first ... or not?! In the following chapters we want to show you what signs of a highly sensitive child can be.

Depending on the age of your child, it is important to know how to deal with high sensitivity. In general, it can be observed that highly sensitive children are often creative minds and act very empathetically. On the other hand, however, they often lack patience and apparent trifles can upset them. If children are generally already impulsive, it is with highly sensitive children to an even greater extent.

2.1. INFANCY

Even babies can be highly sensitive. For example, even rapid changes in light, such as in a tunnel, or even high temperature differences irritate a highly sensitive infant immensely. Highly sensitive infants are incredibly interested in their environment, but remain in an observer role for a very long time. Wanting to explore objects themselves does not seem to be a need of theirs at first.

If the daily routine is not calm and no structure develops, those babies express it all the more through intense crying. This can also happen when you argue with your partner, for example. Those moods are also absorbed by a highly sensitive infant at lightning speed. Perhaps you have already wondered whether your infant is a cry baby. High sensitivity and regulation disorders, which can be found in writing babies, can be connected, but they do not have to be.

Since it is difficult for them to escape stimuli on their own, this is the full responsibility of the parents. Only with increasing mobility is your infant able to move away from "too much" or to communicate to the caregiver with outstretched arms that he or she needs closeness and security. These infants need a lot of physical and emotional attention. It therefore makes sense to carry them in a baby carrier, but under no circumstances facing forward. They would be completely at the mercy of the stimuli and the brain would be overstimulated. Even at larger parties, those babies are very insecure when they wander from arm to arm. It feels most comfortable at home, where it knows all the smells, sounds and also routines. Too many visitors during the postpartum period can have a downright disturbing effect on the very young. If those babies have too few breaks during the day, it is often very difficult for them to fall asleep, as all the impressions have then so overwhelmed the brain that shutting down now means an immense effort. For highly sensitive babies it is so-mit of absolute importance that there is a person who regulates it.

Again and again, one comes across the term "high-need babies" when dealing with sensitive babies or even googling why the child falls asleep so badly in the evening or just wants to be carried. William Sears coined the term high-need babies. He also summarized 12 typical characteristics that make up a high-need baby. They coincide in some points with the questions about highly sensitive children. The fact that there may actually be overlaps here cannot yet be ruled out.

2.2. INFANCY

With increasing age, the characteristic features of high sensitivity become more and more obvious. This is related, for example, to increasing mobility and also language development. The child may withdraw, but he or she may also address situations or changes that you may not have noticed yet. In the toddler age between one and five years, it becomes apparent whether your child is more introverted or extroverted. If your child is already in daycare, he or she will not play much with other children there and will tend to avoid the group as a whole. It may also take months for your child to step out of the observer role and start playing. You may also notice that your daughter or son plays "Kita" at home, but only observes at the Kita itself. This is then simply a processing process.

In infancy, highly sensitive children also stand out for their early and well-developed vocabulary. Both what they can understand and what they say often sets them apart from their peers. The brain is then also so focused and busy on this area of development that other areas such as motor skills are put on hold for the time being.

2.3 THE HIGHLY SENSITIVE CHILD IN THE DAYCARE CENTER

In general, your child can go to any "normal" daycare center. It is up to you to decide whether you want to inform the professionals at the daycare center that your child is highly sensitive. It can be an advantage if the educators are informed about this, so that they can then already act accordingly during the settling-in period and also extend the settling-in period of two weeks if necessary.

If you have only noticed that your child is somehow different from other children, the daycare center can also be an opportunity to find out what this "different" means. Especially in the phase of the observer, the child is observed in his or her everyday life via films and looked at and discussed by the team. Depending on the daycare center concept, you as parents can also be present there and it can be discussed together what your child needs, whether it is highly sensitive and what it shows you in the video. Likewise, those video sequences help the professionals in the case of high sensitivity to work out the small warning signals of the child, in order to enable breaks early enough also in the daycare center and to supplement these to the "usual" breaks such as the nap.

What you could consider when choosing a daycare center would be one that is not too large. There are core groups, but with open concepts, the core groups are exclusively alone at certain times. The rest of the day, each child can move everywhere, which in large houses can be sometimes 60 children and thus an immense effort for a highly sensitive child. If it suits you as a parent, a daycare center with shortened opening hours would also be a possibility, so that your child has enough rest at home and can then also find sleep in the evening in a more relaxed manner.

Be prepared for your child to take longer than the other children to say goodbye in the morning. Highly sensitive children experience this separation as particularly painful. Rituals can also help here; involve the caregiver at the daycare center. A highly sensitive child needs help with transitions, so a specialist must receive the child. If it has been agreed with the daycare center, then take your time for the settling in process. A child who is not well acclimated suffers from stress and a highly sensitive child is then lost. If the daycare center does not meet this special requirement for acclimation, check with the Youth Welfare Office to see if you can change daycare centers for given reasons. It is also possible that you and your child will be assigned an integration assistant.

2.4. SCHOOL AGE

The transition from a daycare child to a schoolchild is per se a special milestone in childhood. Highly sensitive children react particularly intensively to such a drastic change. There are new tasks, new children and also a great deal more responsibility for your child. In addition, the timetables are even stricter, which can of course become a safety hazard. Initially, however, this means stress and pressure. In class, it seems as if highly sensitive children are completely elsewhere with their heads. Even when working on tasks, those children are slower or cannot complete the tasks in class. This can give the impression that the child is not listening properly, does not understand the assignments, and is not smart enough for school. In a quiet, familiar setting like home, none of this is evident. Homework is completed very quickly and conscientiously. In the classroom, too many stimuli are pelting your child so that he or she is unable to concentrate. He or she is busy processing all the information. But if this is too much at some point, they literally beam themselves away or show impulsive, physical behavior, such as rocking on the chair.

2.5 THE HIGHLY SENSITIVE CHILD AT SCHOOL

When the child enters school, the group automatically becomes larger than it was at daycare, and sufficient places of retreat and individual withdrawal times are no longer possible. The advanced age of highly sensitive children at school makes them feel even more different, or even stupid, because they can't keep up with the tasks. But there are so many impressions, after all! Both those impressions and the judgmental feeling inhibit learning. But this does not have to be a permanent condition. With the help of learning therapists, it is possible to give your child the tools to concentrate on learning. Recent research has shown that the combination of physical activity and learning content, coupled with specific brain training, is very promising. Linking both hemispheres of the brain makes learning possible.

It is also advantageous to talk about this with the teachers. For example, it can already help if a highly sensitive child sits in the first rows so that he or she is not crushed by a whole group in front of him or her. These are small changes in everyday life that can have a big effect. Learning therapy and occupational therapy can also be used here.

Another tip: Ask the school if you would be allowed to visit the grounds with your child before enrollment. This will help your child run more accurate images through as he or she prepares internally. It already gives him a first orientation on the first day of school. It can also help if a kindergarten friend goes to the same school and in the same class. More and more schools are offering small retreats right in the classrooms that children are even allowed to use during class. Discuss this with teachers and work together to develop opportunities for smaller breaks for your child. It is also always very helpful if you are in good communication with the teachers. Both to be aware of how your child is doing at school, but also to tell how and in what "condition" the child comes home from school.

Sunny side of high sensitivity

Highly sensitive children often show a strong compassion, act intuitively, are conscientious, their creativity is often very pronounced and it seems to outsiders as if they are very aware of their person. But what does this mean in concrete terms? Often those children are more introverted, but this should not exclude the fact that extroverted children can also be highly sensitive. Highly sensitive children always seem alert to their environment, as if they are constantly on the receiving end and perceive everything. And that is exactly how it is! Every change is perceived. Not infrequently, they also surprise with incredible empathy and can be very fond of animals. P. Tomschi is a board member of the Munich Center for High Sensitivity and likes to use the word "multi-sensitivity" for those children - it doesn't sound so negative anymore.

Another typical feature of highly sensitive children is their attention to detail in questions or answers. They come up with things that adults themselves don't even think of at first. In addition, they are very imaginative and surprise early and untypical for their age with a very good understanding of humor and even irony.

Shadow sides of high sensitivity

The stressful characteristics appear in those children when the brain is overloaded. From one moment to the next, the mood changes - your child can no longer cope, immediately withdraws or becomes loud. This abrupt, initially unpredictable change is often reported by affected parents.

Aggressive behavior can also emerge. For example, they are very susceptible to stress, since even intense smells, the flickering of a defective light bulb, but also cold or a feeling of hunger are borderline for those children. It is therefore imperative that you know the warning signals and harbingers of overstimulation. This way, it is possible to react in time and the mood does not change from one moment to the next.

A lower stimulus threshold also leads to greater sensitivity to pain. Thus, the immune system is more active in these children, so that diseases and allergies occur more frequently. Rejection of certain materials in clothing or consistencies in food can also indicate a highly sensitive child.

Children who are highly sensitive often play alone, as a lot of action quickly overstresses them. Thus, those children are often on the sidelines, watching what is going on or even withdrawing completely and often occupying themselves alone.

2.6 QUESTIONNAIRE FOR CHILDREN

Of course, one can already fill out the questionnaire of E. Aron with children, however, it is warned against it, because one then only imprints a stamp on the child, but could completely overlook it in its uniqueness. However, in order to understand the child and to recognize that it perceives its environment and itself differently and also deals with it differently, such an assessment can be incredibly enriching and also reassuring for parents. The Lower Saxony Institute for Early Childhood Education, abbreviated as NIFBE, has made the questionnaire available on its website for this purpose.

In this test, among other things, questions are asked about sensory perceptions, language vocabulary, contact behavior with other children or also about behavior at parties or larger actions during the day. Even if the test conceptually appears as if it were a test for a diagnosis, it is emphasized that these questions should first of all only lead to an assessment. It is therefore necessary that a pediatrician or even psychological experts are consulted.

The following questions should be answered according to E. Aron in order to get a first assessment of high sensitivity in your child. These questions can also be found in her book "The Highly Sensitive Child":

My child ...

1. startles slightly.
2. has sensitive skin, can not tolerate scratchy fabrics or seams in socks or labels in T-shirts.
3. does not like surprises.
4. benefits in learning through gentle instruction rather than harsh punishment.
5. has an unusually elevated vocabulary for his age.
6. seems to be able to read my mind.
7. is sensitive to odors, even very faint odors.
8. has a clever sense of humor.
9. seems to be very sensitive.
10. can have trouble falling asleep after an exciting day.
11. has trouble with big changes.
12. Finds wet or dirty clothes uncomfortable.
13. asks many questions.
14. is a perfectionist.

15. notices when others are unhappy.

16. prefers quiet games.

17. asks profound questions that make you think.

18. is very sensitive to pain.

19. is sensitive to noise.

20. registers details (changes in a person's furnishings or appearance, etc.).

21. thinks about possible dangers before taking a risk.

22. achieves the best performance when there are no strangers around.

23. has an intense emotional life.

> Evaluation:
> If you can answer "yes" to at least 13 statements, then your child is probably highly sensitive.

It should be emphasized again that this test is not a diagnostic tool. It is only intended to help match impressions and better understand the child.

Unfortunately, high sensitivity is often associated with some kind of weakness in our culture and this is often how those people are treated. They are ostracized or the feeling is conveyed that one must correct this flaw. Being highly sensitive can also lead to a more enjoyable life. The blooming lavender fields, the delicious strawberry cake, the quiet sound of the sea in the evening on the beach, gentle touches while cuddling - everything can be experienced more intensely. In a way that not every person can.

- High sensitivity is already evident in infants.
- A highly sensitive infant is very sensitive to temperature changes, light changes or smells. During play, the infant remains the observer for a very long time, shows great interest, but explores very little.
- Clear daily structures are very important for this infant. Overstimulation they usually express through long and violent crying.
- The more immobile the child, the more responsibility falls on the parents to protect it from too many stimuli.
- In infancy, high sensitivity becomes increasingly evident as the child is mobile and able to express himself linguistically.
- Highly sensitive toddlers show a very mature vocabulary early on.
- Any transition, whether to daycare or school, is stressful for a highly sensitive child.
- In the school setting, the child finds it difficult to stay on task; in the home setting, the child completes tasks accurately and without difficulty.
- There is a questionnaire to assess possible high sensitivity.

The next chapter will deal with what it means to be a parent of a highly sensitive child. First, you as a parent will be addressed, what it means for you and what process is triggered when you deal with the assumption "Our child is highly sensitive". After that, it is concretely about advice for the everyday interaction with your child - both what is good for your child, but also what is inappropriate for your highly sensitive child.

3. being a parent of a highly sensitive child

Everyday life with a highly sensitive child can be very challenging. Since the threshold of irritation is crossed very quickly and often, it can also significantly more often lead to restlessness and stress for all involved. The following tips will show you how you can shape parenting.

However, before we take a closer look at those tips from Elaine Aron, I invite you to a short mental excursion. Let's try to experience what your child is experiencing, and only in terms of one sense for now. Many stimuli are so normal for us that we pass over them. Therefore, put on your ears and listen to the room you are in right now. What do you hear? Which sounds are loud, which are quiet, which are more unpleasant than others? And do you really only hear the noises in this room or are there enough also from the street outside, from the kitchen and, and, and? All that you now hear under conscious focus and concentration, your highly sensitive child hears all the time. And in addition to all these sounds, there are also smells, visual and tactile stimuli, etc. - a potpourri of impressions.

Elaine Aron has summarized tips on how to first deal with the suspicion that your child may be highly sensitive. These will now be listed and explained.

Recognize high sensitivity
First of all, familiarize yourself with the terminology. Google it, talk to people like psychologists, a doctor or associations - a contact point where you can dock with all your questions. There are a wide variety of characteristics in highly sensitive people. Nevertheless, according to E. Aron, at some point there is a moment when it "CLICKS" with the parents and you recognize your child in the listed characteristics. Suddenly, stones fall from your heart because there are finally

explanations for what you intuitively noticed in your child. And that can be immensely relieving!

Critically consider

Due to the variety of combinations of characteristics for high sensitivity, doubts may continue to arise in you. This process is natural and should encourage you to remain curious. New things must first be questioned so that they can become a consolidated basis. It is essential for your child that you look, listen and read carefully. Only then will you be able to recognize the individual expression in your child and, depending on the expression, you will be able to create space and possibilities for your child, which he or she needs for recovery. High sensitivity must also be lived out in the same way as, for example, a high urge to move. If there are no opportunities for this, similar patterns can emerge as in children with mental disorders.

A common critical question from parents is also "everyone is sensitive". Yes, that is true. But this is based on a learned empathy, which we experienced and learned in childhood in the social environment. High sensitivity is innate and differs from being sensitive and acting sensitive in the lack of filtering of external stimuli. Smells, voices, gestures - all this is taken in unfiltered. Whether the child wants it or not. It just happens.

This incomprehensible breadth and variety of information then gives rise to a pronounced empathy.

It may be that your child has a peculiarity in relation to a certain color or material of clothing, etc.. This can sometimes become very stressful. However, try to remember that this is not out of defiance or provocation. Your child also feels things differently on the skin. A seam on the cap can not only be annoying, but also very uncomfortable. Or the washing paper not only rubs against the back of the neck, no, for your child it itches terribly and then rustles with every movement of the head. This may sound banal, but for your child it is not. If you can take these particular idiosyncrasies into account in everyday life and eliminate these inconveniences, it will be much more pleasant for you and your child. You are not spoiling your child in this case, you are responding to his need. After all, if we felt that the size label was itching on the back of our necks, we would cut it out as well. Your child will thank you and learn once again how to deal with himself and his needs in life. It feels seen by you! And that strengthens immensely!

Obtain information
Get information. It doesn't matter whether it's via the Internet, by attending a group of affected parents, or

even via a coaching or counseling session for parents. Knowledge makes it easier and also hearing how other families are doing and how their everyday lives are going can be immensely helpful and provide the necessary psychological hygiene. A conversation with an expert can also clarify many questions and uncertainties, especially in the beginning. The "High Sensitivity Network" offers valuable literature tips on its website as well as the possibility to find consultants in your environment. There is also an online platform with information events, a regulars' table and meetings for relatives and also those affected themselves.

There is also the possibility of watching films or documentaries in general on the subject. A small selection of these would be the following films:

- The anonymous romantics
- Proud to be Sensitive
- The Supermen.

New look at your child
Allow your child to guide you a little. It is assumed that newborns are already competent. And they are competent at teaching their parents sensitive behavior. Through their different tones and facial expressions,

infants show your parents that something is wrong. What it always is then is up to you to find out. Gradually, attentive caregivers can recognize what their child needs by subtle nuances.

A highly sensitive child can also help you to reconnect. It may happen that you look back into the past and feel guilty because certain moments are now also in a different light and you wish you had the info about high sensitivity earlier. But don't get stuck on those memories. You know it now and you can now start to rebuild your relationship with your child. This is wonderful! It will also require certain efforts and a lot of patience from all involved, nevertheless, in the best case you will be able to perceive, accompany and finally encourage your child's specialness. In this way, your child will gain self-confidence and, moreover, confidence in you. After all, it no longer needs to worry that being different is stupid, because at home it can show itself with its whole personality and thus also reveal more and more to you, show strengths, which you in turn can respond to. Here it becomes clear once again that this mutual relationship for both parties always has learning potential for the other. Your child learns from you and you from your child.

Common questions

There are a few questions that are on the minds of most parents. Among others, the following are the most frequently asked questions and the ones that come to mind and burn under the nails the quickest.

Does the diagnosis "highly sensitive child" exist? - Even though there are questionnaires and some studies on this topic, a pathological diagnosis is not yet possible. This is due to the so far inaccessible criteria that allow an objective diagnosis.

Is high sensitivity a disease? - No. High sensitivity is a character trait. Your child is not ill or disturbed.

Of course, there will and can be many more questions floating around in your head. This is normal and part of the process. After all, you are dealing with the subject matter. If your own research does not provide you with sufficiently satisfactory answers, you can again use experts, doctors, concerned parents or even associations.

3.1 WHAT DOES MY HIGHLY SENSITIVE CHILD?

Your child will very quickly recognize that he or she is different from other children and even adults. It can therefore recognize this very early because it senses it so sensitively. Since the majority of everyday life is not designed for highly sensitive people, this can make a child doubt itself very quickly. You as parents have a very responsible role to play here. With which possibilities and tips you can accompany and strengthen your child, will now be shown.

3.2 MOVING AWAY FROM EDUCATION TO RELATIONSHIP

First of all: The fact that your child feels so much is a special feature. Recognizing and respecting this should be your basic attitude in your relationship with your child. Do not try to change your child, but try to let your child show you his special world of perception and processing, as far as this is possible.

Perhaps you have already turned to classic parenting guides and realized that they don't really apply to your child or don't "bear fruit". Since your child ticks a little differently, you also need a different suitcase of handling tips. For this suitcase, it is best to first go on an observation tour: What does your child like to play with and how does he play with it? When does he need your help? When do you notice that fixed rituals do your child good and does he or she perhaps even demand them? What is the first thing your child does after school? These are just a few examples of how you can observe your child in everyday life. How you can continue to shape everyday life and what you could pay attention to if your child is highly sensitive will now be shown again in more detail.

A needs-oriented upbringing is particularly beneficial for highly sensitive children - and for parents as well. After all, the point is that all needs in the family have their right to exist. A needs-oriented relationship does not mean that the child gets everything he or she apparently wants. It is about recognizing and acknowledging the needs and then acting on them. The younger the child, the more prompt the response, because a newborn has only very essential needs that should not be postponed. Closeness, food, sleep, fresh diaper - for newborns, it feels like complete helplessness if these needs are not met.

Attitude plays an important role. The children are not assumed to have a bad intention, but a need is always seen behind it. Even a defiant, angry child has a need, and be it the need for a boundary, a hold or a decision, which in turn coincides with the behavior of an overstimulated, highly sensitive child. Thus, needs-based parenting is not about the child being able to do whatever he or she wants. Where would be the structure, the hold-giving daily routine, the rituals? It is about respect towards the other, one renounces punishments, communicates facts, there are family rules for all family members and best of all these have been compiled by the whole family. In this way, the whole family is also involved when it comes to boundaries. Such an educational model strengthens the children in their social behavior and also builds their self-confidence at the same time. In the family environment, they can experience and practice how to interact respectfully and at eye level with other people, whether at daycare, school or even at work.

3.3 REFERENCE PERSONS AS ANCHOR

A stable relationship with confidants is also of immense importance for highly sensitive children. Take your child seriously. It will still happen often enough that people doubt your child's perception, be it teachers, other children or even friends and family. This can cause your child to begin doubting himself and his perceptions as well. Believe your child when he or she tells you about his or her feelings, because this is reality for your son or daughter. Don't be afraid to ask or have him or her describe how something looked, smelled, or felt. In the situations themselves, watch for disapproving gestures, facial expressions, and other nonverbal communication patterns. Then first try to give the child a break. Give him a hug, offer comfort, cuddle with him or look at a book.

Over time, you will find out which path your child can use to calm down. Then go to the cause research - what was the trigger? You could also try keeping a diary, as you do for people with migraines. What was going on that day when your child became overwhelmed? Was something different than usual? Were there any behaviors of your child's that slowly built up on each other that you could have noticed were starting to get to be too much for him? When did you notice that it was getting to be too much? How did your child react? But then again, what helped your child relax?

If your child can already talk, just ask him or her. Name possible feelings that your child might have felt and at what moment which feeling became quite powerful. Once the trigger is found, you can think about whether it is avoidable next time or whether you can find a way for and also with your child to make the trigger more bearable. This can mean, for example, that you first stay with the child for the entire hour of gymnastics and then withdraw step by step - similar to settling in at daycare.

It also helps your highly sensitive child a lot if you explain to him or her in advance what to expect, for example, during a visit to the doctor. Perhaps you can playfully go through what the doctor will do with your child beforehand. Also, when you travel, you may find that your child first has to warm up to the new surroundings, the new impressions. Familiar objects from home and consistent rituals, such as going to bed, can make it easier for your child to arrive in a different environment. Secure attachment figures with their support-giving function, sometimes even to be taken literally, serve as anchors and points of orientation.

One field that opens up in people with high sensitivity is the incredibly great empathy. A child who is highly sensitive already feels the feelings of others as his or her own feelings. This confluence of feelings must be addressed, as your child should learn to protect himself from it. Each feeling may and must remain with the person who feels it, and your child must learn that he or she may be quietly happy even if he or she senses that someone else is not happy at the moment. If you notice that your child also gets physical problems due to his high sensitivity, such as frequent headaches, stomach aches, little appetite, little sleep, please contact your pediatrician and a psychotherapist. Even adults find it difficult from time to time to set boundaries for their own good. Recognize this in your child at an early stage and accompany him/her in recognizing and standing up for his/her own boundaries and feelings.

To talk to your child about their high sensitivity, there are now great picture books and books for adolescents. After all, it helps that your child himself also understands what it is that feels so different about him. Also, picture books can be used to relate to your child and open a new door.

The following (picture) books, among others, deal with the topic of high sensitivity:

- "I am the way I am - brilliant and totally normal" by Sabina Pilguj
- "The Worry Animal - What's it like for you?" by Christina Wagner-Meisterburg.
- "The Lion in You" by Rachel Bright and Jim Field.
- "Thousand-Sensitivity Lars: Children with High Sensitivity" by Hannah-Marie Heine

- "Enno Anders: Dandelions in the Asphalt" by Astrid Frank.

3.4 NO-GOS IN THE RELATION-SHIP WITH YOUR HIGHLY SENSI-TIVE CHILD

Take your child seriously! What he or she feels, he or she feels and this cannot and must not be downplayed, ignored or devalued. If your child asks you to walk on the other side of the street because the sun is so blinding or so hot, your child feels it more intensely than you do. Yes, you will need a lot of patience, and yes, there are bound to be phrases like "now, don't be a pain" on your lips from time to time.

Perhaps it will help you to keep reminding yourself that your child really does feel what he or she is telling you and showing you. The fact that it tells you this at all shows that it trusts you and also helps you to understand your child and also to recognize possible triggers for overstimulation at an early stage. In the most extreme case, your child will otherwise experience that his feelings are not taken seriously, he will doubt himself and lose access to himself. Even in adulthood, highly sensitive people who experienced the described type in childhood have very great difficulties in perceiving their own needs and feelings at all. They are immediately denied, suppressed and ignored.

3.5 WHAT DOES MY CHILD NEED IN EVERYDAY LIFE?

Strengthen self-confidence

Because of the frequent feeling of being "different," it is of immense importance to build and stabilize your child's self-esteem. Generalized threats should be avoided, as with any child. Start with yourself and be a role model for your child with your exemplified self-respect. Always take a look at the advantages your child experiences through his or her gift and try to refrain from comparisons with other children. Your child will be able to cope better if you notice that he or she is perhaps tired now and would prefer to leave, but you briefly tell him or her that you still need 5 minutes, but that he or she can sit in the car or something similar.

Support contact with peers

A boy who is highly sensitive finds it particularly difficult to get into contact with peers who just love to romp and scuffle. Of course, there are also difficulties for highly sensitive girls in contact with other children.

One possibility would be to let the child learn something special, so that he/she strengthens his/her self-confidence and feels competent. Role-playing games can also help your child deal with his or her worries and playfully experience how to make friends with other children.

But how could you now find out which child might fit your child? You are not there in the day care center or school. For this purpose, however, simply ask the caregivers or teachers. They will be the first to make contact. This would allow the two children to do something together in the afternoon. It could be that your child wants to go home after two hours or needs a break. But that's perfectly fine. The more familiar the friendship becomes, the more relaxed your child can be and the two children can settle down.

Often, children still play a sport or instrument on the weekend or during the week in the afternoon. A team sport is a great challenge, but has many advantages for your child. Since it is all about the sport and the performance, integration into the group can happen well. Studies in the U.S. have shown that highly sensitive boys who participated in a team sport were well received and received little to no teasing. Find out together with your child which sport he or she could imagine participating in, attend a few sessions there, and then consider together with your child where he or she felt comfortable and where he or she could imagine participating again.

Stimulus Reduction

If your child has experienced a lot during the day, the evening is often very restless and the child is jittery. When the body comes to rest, the mind is still processing. It is therefore all the more important that it is completely quiet when falling asleep, no stars projected on the ceiling and your child, regardless of age, can find peace without further stimuli.

The range of toys should also be looked at carefully. Highly sensitive babies play differently. Too many impressions are exhausting and intuitively the baby tends to occupy himself with few, but challenging toys. Since they are very curious and attentive, they like challenging play. Do not overwhelm your child with toys, avoid continuous sound or a continuous crowd of visitors. Yes, children are spellbound by bright colors and flashing toys. The younger your child is, the less of such toys you should offer your child. And again, though, it's important not to exclude your child from everything. In the end, it is much more a matter of shaping everyday life together with the child so that he or she is part of society and also experiences how to deal with his or her special talent.

For school children doing homework, care should be taken to ensure that there are no additional sources of noise in the environment. The radio should be off, no side conversations in the kitchen when the child is doing his or her chores at the dining room table. Less is more.

In terms of playmates, your child will also benefit more from a few friends than from a whole horde. Invite a child over once in a while, but don't push your child. Likewise, an afternoon activity such as gymnastics or the like can be attended. However, don't be disappointed if it takes longer for you and your child to find a suitable activity. Patience and composure are needed here. Get your child fit for life and let him or her inspire you.

Rituals for psychological security

Structured daily routines and clearly recognizable rules are generally an important component for children. Everything that is known and always runs in a similar way gives security and the feeling of being in control and also being able to switch off and be allowed to switch off. For highly sensitive children, this means that their brains are not working at full capacity all the time, but that they can fall back on familiar information that they have already experienced. Rituals, rules and structures thus become a kind of pre-sorting by the outside, by you as parents.

Breaks

You may already have noticed that your child is very flat or also very hyper or even aggressive at home after a day at school or kindergarten. School and daycare are full of stimuli. Try not to cram the afternoon too full of activities, but allow your child to rest. You could also work with your child to design an area or corner in his or her nursery in such a way that it becomes the optimal retreat for the child and contributes to his or her rest. In this way, your child will also feel serious and noticed and will be able to meet his needs.

Now, this is not meant to give the impression of not offering your child club sports or anything similar. It is simply a matter of setting fixed times during the day when your child can relax. You cannot protect your child from all stimuli and a stimulus overload can also have a positive purpose from time to time: you and your child experience that and how one can find one's way out of such a situation again. Likewise, withdrawal should not become isolation from the environment. Loneliness makes people ill. Nevertheless, care should be taken to ensure that overstimulation is not a permanent condition, as stress is not healthy for the body. Therefore, it is recommended to be considerate with the child, but not to overbrowbeat.

Know warning signals

It is especially important for parents to recognize the individual signals of impending overstimulation in their children.

The following behaviors may indicate that things are getting too much for your child:
- Whining
- Retreat
- Nothing more to speak
- Whining
- Inevitably seek physical contact, extend your arms to you
- Abdominal pain, headache, aching limbs.

Since stress also has a direct effect on the body, your child may complain of abdominal pain if he or she has "too much". This should be taken seriously. For example, put on a hot water bottle and relax with your child. Likewise, massages can also be pleasantly relaxing. The child feels itself again and that is good. There are also highly sensitive children who find it helpful to be outside in the forest.

If your child exhibits one or more of these behaviors, you should allow your child a recovery period. If your child is already overwhelmed, you can no longer ask him to make decisions. You will probably have to decide whether your child wants to relax by reading a book or by cuddling. Anger and aggression inhibit any rational decision-making - take this task away from your child. You now restore order to your child's inner chaos. And this can be both external order and internal order. Verbalize what you are going to do now, why you are doing it and also talk about your child's feelings. Avoid harsh words and try not to scold.

Ultimately, it is always a matter of finding out what applies to your child and what behavior he or she shows when something becomes too much for him or her. But this is also true for parents whose children are not highly sensitive. Get involved with your child and be attentive to what your child is trying to tell you. Stay in contact with him or her and talk about feelings that you perceive in your child, but also in yourself. Feel free to make assumptions about how your child is doing, how you perceive him or her, and what you think might be good for him or her to recover.

3.6 OVERSTRAINING THE PARENTS

It can be exhausting when you have a highly sensitive child. And you are allowed to admit that! Even children who are not highly sensitive can mean stressful times for parents at some point. There is no shame in that. Still, it's important to recognize when it's getting to be too much for you or you notice that you're not doing well anymore, because a worn-out mom or dad doesn't do the child any good either. Little energy also quickly exhausts your patience and your behavior is then sometimes no longer completely rational towards the child. Your highly sensitive child senses something like this immediately.

So don't be afraid to talk about it and to say that you are reaching your limits. Batteries can run down and need to be recharged first. Maybe you can find out what could do you good to recharge your batteries. What are you missing? What would you need? Is there something you could do immediately? Would it take half a day all to yourself?

Also banish the guilty conscience when your partner offers to take your child for half a day and do something together. You can think together about what the two of you could experience and what your husband might have to pay attention to in that case. Especially working parents do not notice many of the everyday hurdles of highly sensitive children and are then also grateful for tips.

Accept support. Your child has nothing to gain from a mom or dad who can no longer do anything. Sometimes a massage can also help, which you can have prescribed by your family doctor.

From time to time, it can also help to talk to other parents in the same situation. On the Internet you can find some groups and forums that offer space for exchange. So it is no longer bound to only one support group and depending on the type you can decide which kind of exchange suits you more.

If you do find that all of these options are not helping you and the batteries just won't recharge, don't be afraid to ask your family doctor for therapeutic help. It could be a few sessions with a therapist or even a cure. In any case, you should also allow yourself to be looked after.

> - Being a parent of a highly sensitive child is exhausting.

- If your child is indeed highly sensitive, start with yourself. You need to restructure your thoughts. Try to perceive your child, get information, exchange information with other families.
- Your child will notice very quickly that he or she is different from the other children. Get into a relationship with your child and address the issue together.
- Moving away from education to relationships.
- Talking about feelings, watching picture books and movies, role-playing to prepare for appointments - become a team.
- Reduce stimuli, recognize warning signals of over-stimulation, introduce rituals, allow breaks in everyday life.
- Take your child and his perception seriously - he feels differently than you, but he feels that way.
- You are the orientation and anchor for your child.
- Take care of yourself, too! A worn-out mother or a tired father is of little use to his children. You, too, are allowed to take time out.

4. will my child have problems all his life? have?

Your child will not be troubled for the rest of his or her life. But to reach this state, it is important to explore and try out strategies with your child to take good care of him or herself in stressful moments, to discover and consolidate resources. Especially in areas of work where a lot of empathy is needed, highly sensitive people can use their gift very well. Likewise, they are often very good at negotiating and settling disputes without stepping on anyone's toes. If there is a problem somewhere, they are able to perceive all aspects around it and to form a suitable solution from it, in the best case very fairly for all involved. One should not exclude the possibility that highly sensitive people can also assume leadership positions. Since work is particularly accurate, a job in the area of quality management is just as suitable. The great empathy is also very helpful in social areas and working with animals.

Your child can have a very wonderful and valuable life, don't worry about that. The high sensitivity can even be the special feature that positively stands out and is seen as the added value for a team.

Concluding Impulses

Rolf Sellin is the director of the Institute for Highly Sensitive Persons in Stuttgart. He calls children with high sensitivity a gift. He clearly sees this as a strength and even for society as a whole.

Be brave! Your child is something special. If you get involved, your child will show you the world with all its senses and impressions. You are invited to look at things in a new way and also to set new priorities. Yes, your child perceives more than perhaps you do. This can also be scary if your own child is always one step ahead of the parents in some ways. But it may also be a great enrichment for your family. You may also experience the world in a completely different way or slow down the entire family routine.

How often do you go beyond your own physical and mental limits, which on the one hand can also be useful, but in the permanent state drains and moves you far away from yourself. The relationship to oneself, to perceive one's own needs again and again and to classify them as justified, is healthy and is often too seldom consciously demanded. Perhaps your highly sensitive child will help you with this. If your child needs a break, then simply use the time together or with your other children. Then it will no longer feel like an individual measure for your highly sensitive child and everyone will literally move closer together.

You will experience feelings of relief, fear, amazement, overwhelm and much more. Everything is allowed and normal. You are not alone and there are places to go to help you and your family find out if your child is indeed highly sensitive and what you and your family need in terms of information, support and also relief. Starting over after the realization can take a weight of uncertainty off your shoulders, but it can also mean a mountain of restructuring and work. The readjustment requires a lot of energy, but it will settle down and become the norm. I wish you much success and strength in this and think it is wonderful that you are setting out on this path. For your child, for you, for your whole family.